GET IT RIGHT
THE FIRST TIME

THE OWNER-MANAGER'S
GUIDE TO HIRING A CFO

Lance Osborne

ISBN 978-0-9938213-8-7 (paperback)
ISBN 978-0-9938213-9-4 (ePUB)

Cover design, and typesetting:
Daniel Crack, Kinetics Design, kdbooks.ca

Printed in Canada

CONTENTS

Introduction

If you're like most of my clients, you actively dislike the process of recruiting for your executive team. And if you're a typical owner-manager, you especially dislike having to hire a CFO. As much as recruiting a sales or operations executive is no walk in the park, at least you have a detailed understanding of those functions and are probably pretty confident that you'll be able to identify the right candidate when they walk through the door.

However, many owner-managers don't have as detailed an understanding or appreciation for the finance function and are less comfortable when it comes to hiring a CFO. Since most owner-managers come from outside the finance and accounting community, many of the questions they should be asking – questions around education and designation, scope of position, performance metrics and even title – are not raised.

Exacerbating the problem is that, for many owner-managed enterprises, the CFO role can be a moving target. Strictly speaking, the title Chief

Financial Officer just refers to the person responsible for overseeing the financial activities of a company. This person could be the Vice President of Finance or they could be the Director of Finance. In many owner-managed businesses, the Controller is the de facto CFO. These positions are quite different in scope and function, but any of the individuals holding these positions can act as the CFO.

The CFO function typically evolves as a function of the company's growth in size and sophistication. Having a Controller as the CFO may be entirely appropriate for a company at one stage, but as the company grows in size, complexity and ambition, the CFO role will be better served by a Director or Vice President of Finance.

In either case, having the right person in the top finance chair can make a very big contribution to the overall success of your business. Once you've hired your first CFO, the first thing you'll notice is that you have a lot of extra hours in the week to dedicate to revenue-generating activities. Insurance, administration, information technology, human resources, facilities management – all of these activities could and should roll under your CFO.

This e-book will discuss the factors and issues you need to consider when it comes time to hire a CFO for your organization. We'll talk about accounting designations (pre- and post-CPA merger) and explain how one designation may be more appropriate to your business than the others. We'll differentiate between the Controller, Director of Finance and Vice President of Finance roles and give some guidelines on what position would be the most appropriate for your business. We'll also discuss how to tie compensation to objective performance metrics. And finally, we'll discuss the principles and best practices you'll need to employ when recruiting for a CFO.

Recruiting and hiring the right person for your top finance position will have a big impact on the overall success of your business. When it comes to hiring your CFO, you not only want to get it right – you want to get it right the first time out.

1

Why You Should Avoid the Path of Least Resistance

Some time ago I met with the executives of a $40-million automotive service company to discuss recruiting a CFO for their business. The owner-managers were the sons of the company's founder, and the reason they wanted to conduct a CFO search was to replace someone who was essentially the Controller. The incumbent had been with the company for over 30 years and was planning on retiring. The owner-managers had plans to build on the success that the company had already enjoyed and were taking the incumbent's retirement as an opportunity to recruit a qualified CFO to help them implement their growth strategy.

The executive team had grown up in the business and were very savvy operators. They understood that in order to properly realize their growth potential they needed to fill out their executive ranks with someone who would bring a higher level of financial sophistication and business acumen to the table.

We talked about the company's history, its current growth trajectory and the plans the brothers had to expand their reach in their market. After we had done a deep dive into the state of their operations and plans for growth, we mapped out the functionality of what would essentially be a new position and talked at length about what the new CFO should look like. The owners were very detailed and specific about technical qualifications, industry experience, management style and potential to grow with the company.

After about two hours, we had thoroughly scoped out the position and agreed on a candidate profile that would meet the company's current requirements and fit with their future plans. As this was a family owned and operated enterprise, we paid special attention to the personality profile of prospective candidates. In a search like this, technical and professional qualifications and experience are table stakes. What really determines the success of the hire is the personality fit, and not just with the owner-managers. In companies where the owners have grown up in the business, and the management and senior staff have worked together for many years, anyone joining the executive team needs to mesh well with everyone.

After the meeting I sent out a proposal and started thinking about how we would approach this assignment. I hadn't heard back on my proposal for a couple of weeks and so I called the owners to ask what was up. They explained that they hadn't pulled the trigger yet because someone they knew referred a CPA to them who was looking for a new position, and they wanted to take a look at him before they started the search.

Needless to say, this turned out to be the person they hired to be their CFO.

I'm pretty sure the company didn't make a bad hire. The referral was a CPA, probably had experience as a VP Finance and, if the company owners had decided to hire them, they obviously got along. But, and this is a big "but," I'm also pretty sure that they didn't make the right hire. The owner-managers had a well-thought-out list of criteria that they felt were necessary for any prospective CFO to succeed in the position. The odds of finding those criteria in a random referral are very, very remote. However, the person they hired did have one very big thing going for them – they were convenient.

As often happens with owner-managers who need to a hire a CFO, the brothers were faced with the proverbial fork in the road. On one side was the road marked "Full Blown Search," a path they knew was both time consuming and expensive. On the other side was the road marked "Least Resistance," a path that was both quick and cheap.

I'm sure the brothers knew that a full-blown search would produce better results than the quick-and-easy fix; but as is often the case with owner-managers who are hiring a CFO for the first time, they didn't think that the extra time and expense justified the incremental difference in outcomes. However, in many if not most cases, the incremental difference in outcomes to your business can range anywhere from significant to game changing.

In my experience, CEOs who've previously had a top-notch finance professional on their executive team appreciate the value a good CFO brings to the table. They are always willing to take the time, trouble and expense entailed in hiring the best person for the job every time they're on the market for a CFO.

Owner-managers who are a hiring a CFO for the first time or who don't really have an appreciation for the value a good finance executive brings to the table tend to think that all accountants are created equal. These are the people that usually take the path of least resistance when they need to recruit a CFO; relying on referrals and job boards to produce the candidate they'll ultimately end up hiring. The assumption here is if someone has their CPA designation and some experience as a VP Finance, they're a viable candidate for the job.

Although there's no data available on the outcomes resulting from this type of process, I suspect that the 20/60/20 rule comes into play: 20% of the hires will be failures, 60% will be average to pretty good fits and 20% will be top performers.

There are two major implications to the statement above. First, the odds are stacked against you hiring a top performer. Your most probable outcome is that you'll hire someone who's okay, but not a star (and of course you run a real risk of making a bad hire). And second, you'll end up paying anyone you hire about the same as you would have paid a top performer. But even if many owner-managers don't fully appreciate what a great CFO hire brings to the table, they'll all recognize what a bad hire takes off the table.

A Cautionary Tale

I once had a client that habitually took the path of least resistance when they hired CFOs. After hiring and firing three CFOs in rapid succession, they came to me for help. We did a comprehensive review of the position and what the CEO wanted to achieve, and agreed upon a very specific candidate profile. Further, the client and I agreed that this time out, he would follow my advice and adopt the best practices that would result in a good hire. The most critical of the best practices that we agreed upon was that the client would interview at least four well-qualified candidates before taking anyone to the next step of the process.

My team and I were about three weeks into the project when we got a call from the client: he had had someone referred to him whom he thought was a good candidate. "No problem," I replied, "let's just throw that candidate into the mix and we'll come up with the rest of the short list so you have a choice." (Ironically, it turned out that the person referred was someone that I had already interviewed in the course of the search and had decided not to present.)

As you've probably already guessed, the client wouldn't take my advice. He was too busy to interview other candidates and, in any event, didn't want to wait the extra time it would take to pull together a full short list. And besides, the person referred to him was unemployed and available to start right away. (This is almost always the case when someone hires on the path of least resistance. They want someone who'll start solving their problem now, not two or three months from now.)

He ran the candidate through their process and sure enough, had a new CFO in place a few weeks later.

Fast forward eight months and my client was in a world of hurt. The Controller had one foot out the door (which would have been a very bad thing as he was the only person in finance with any institutional memory), a number of the finance department staff had quit, the management team had lost all confidence in the finance department and the owners of the company were very unhappy that none of the objectives the CFO was hired to achieve had been advanced in any way.

And, to top it all off, the CFO had just resigned, giving a scant two weeks' notice.

I've seen bad hires like this before, but what stands out about this bad hire is not just the amount of damage this person caused but how quickly it all happened. Usually, bad hires are much slower train wrecks and the damage usually plays out over 12 to 18 months before the CEO has had enough and finally pulls the trigger. The other unusual component of this case was that the CFO jumped and wasn't pushed. Which brings me to another hazard of hiring the convenient, unemployed candidate – flight risk.

I mentioned earlier that we had interviewed this person and had decided not to put him on the short list. The main reason was that he was actually much too senior for the job. My client was a $60-million entrepreneurial manufacturer going through a lot of growth and change that needed someone who would be very hands-on. The person they hired had been the CFO of a $1-billion division of a multi-national and had been making a lot more than the client wanted to pay.

My first concern was that this person wouldn't be hands-on enough (among other things). My second concern was the compensation. Even though the client ended up paying this person quite a bit more than they had planned, it was still quite a bit less than this person was making before.

Unemployed executives are often not negotiating from a position of strength and can sometimes feel compelled to take a lesser job at lesser pay just to stop the bleeding. In some cases it works out for both parties. However, in many cases after the first year or so on the job, that person starts to act on the impulse to get back to the level they operated at before. In this case, it turned out that my client's ex-CFO landed a job very similar to his previous position at what I presume was a similar level of compensation.

A bad hire like this one is relatively rare. The more common threat to owner-managed enterprises is the below average CFO. Many owner-managers don't have an adequate yardstick to measure the capability of their top finance person. If their CFO doesn't happen to be up to snuff, they run a real risk of being blindsided.

For example, I had one client who bought all of his product in the U.S. and all of his customers were in Canada. The Canadian dollar went from $1.03 USD in 2007 to $0.79 USD by 2009, and my client had no foreign exchange hedges in place. This had a serious impact on the health of my client's business and could have been easily avoided had the right CFO been in place.

Occupying the biggest stretch of the range between good and bad CFO hires is the average CFO. They'll get the job done competently and they won't cause you any grief. Neither will they have a material, positive impact on the success of your business. And as I pointed out previously, you're going to pay the average person about the same as you pay the high performer. In effect, you're paying for steak and getting hamburger.

Avoid taking the path of least resistance when it comes time to hire a CFO. In the end, it will turn out to be the more expensive option by far. Take the time and trouble (and expense) to do it right and you'll have someone in your top finance spot who will have a positive impact on your business.

Straight Answers to Real Questions:

► ### Value for Money

Question: I run a $70-million manufacturing business out in Mississauga. My CFO just quit and I need to find a replacement. Frankly, I'm not sorry to see this guy go. He never really added a lot of value other than keeping the accounting function going smoothly. He was with me 10 years and I was paying him a base salary of $190,000, plus a bonus based on company profitability. I'm ready to take the company to the next level and I think a really sharp finance executive could help me get there. If I pay the next Vice President of Finance a whole lot more, will I get a whole lot more bang for my buck?

Answer: I'm a firm believer that you end up getting what you pay for. That being said, you shouldn't have to overpay to find what you need. A base of $190,000 plus bonus seems reasonable for a company of your size; it sounds like you just weren't getting what you paid for. Unless you're anticipating that you'll be experiencing exponential growth, you don't need to up the ante significantly to recruit a really effective Vice President of Finance.

The market for financial executives is fairly evenly traded – people tend to get paid what they're worth. There are two common factors in the recruitment process that lead to overpaying for an underperforming asset: (1) not having well-thought-out, properly defined expectations for the position, and (2) looking at too-small a field of candidates. If you take the time to really nail down what you need this position to accomplish and benchmark what the market for financial executives in this space looks like, you are much more likely to hire a financial executive who will give you proper value for your money.

2

How Much Horsepower Do You Need?

When Do You Need to Hire a CFO?

When owner-managed companies start out, their accounting needs are few and relatively simple. Cheques need to be cut, invoices need to be collected, people need to get paid, the government needs its taxes and so forth. Actually, most of what needs to be done in the name of accounting could be categorized as bookkeeping. That's why owner-managers usually start out hiring someone who knows bookkeeping to handle the company's accounting function.

Bookkeeping is simply the clerical function of recording a business's day-to-day operations, and for owner-managers of many small companies, that's usually all that's required. By virtue of the fact that most owner-managers of small companies are intimately involved with all aspects of their company's operations, they don't need someone to tell them how they're doing in the marketplace or how much raw materials have gone up in price in the past 12 months. They're talking to their customers regularly and they remember how much their suppliers were charging last year.

But as a company starts enjoying success, it's not just its revenues that grow; everything gets bigger. And an increase in size usually means an increase in complexity in office and plant facilities, capital expenditures, customer base, sales and marketing activities, goods and services offered, etc. This increased complexity means that the owner-manager can no longer keep their eye on every moving ball. That's when they need their bookkeeping function to evolve into an accounting department.

As the collection of data, organization of information and sophistication of reporting required by management becomes correspondingly complex, owner-managers need to hire someone to oversee the finance/accounting function. While it varies from industry to industry, there are usually four factors that lead business owners to the decision to hire a CFO:

Size & Complexity: As companies get bigger, there's usually an increased complexity in physical plant, inventories, service contracts, supplier and customer deliverables, capital expenditures and so on. Someone needs to oversee the recording and organization of all this information and provide meaningful reports to senior management.

Growth: Any substantive growth, and especially rapid growth, benefits from automated systems to handle the growth. Growing companies often require appropriate financing to underwrite their growth. A qualified CFO will be able to invest in and implement the requisite information technology systems and get access to additional capital.

Acquisitions: Growing companies often face any number of decisions around acquisitions of other companies, lines of business or physical plants. A CFO can put together the right team to evaluate these transactions and make a recommendation around their viability and impact on current and future operations. The CFO is also able to prepare the information required by a potential lender or investor to fund the transaction.

Credibility: Last but not least, having a qualified CFO in place can be critical when respect is required by various inside and outside stakeholders. Such stakeholders could include shareholders, suppliers, customers, bankers or regulators.

Vice President of Finance, Director of Finance or Controller?

In owner-managed companies, the person responsible for overseeing the finance function is invariably the CFO. However, they don't necessarily carry the title of VP Finance. In fact, in most owner-managed companies, the top financial person is not a VP Finance. More commonly, they are a Director of Finance or sometimes the Controller.

Once you've made the decision that you need a qualified professional to head up your finance function, the next decision is determining how much horsepower you actually need in your CFO. And in order to do that, you need to realistically assess not only how much technical horsepower is required to handle the job but also how much operational input you actually need (and will take) from your top finance person.

Someone who just wants timely and accurate accounting and financial reporting, adequate internal controls, management reports and some operational input at the department head level should probably hire a Controller. The owner-manager who wants all of those functions looked after plus meaningful input on operations and strategic decisions should look for someone with the experience of a Vice President of Finance.

A good rule of thumb is that the Controller function is basically backward-looking. Their purview is capturing financial information that reflects the past and informs the present. The Vice President of Finance function is forward-looking. A good VP Finance helps the CEO and executive team at a high operational and strategic level and can often anticipate potential problems or identify opportunities that might not otherwise be recognized.

More often than not, owner-managed enterprises require someone with the hands-on accounting skills of a Controller coupled with the heads-up strategic and forward-looking qualities of a Vice President of Finance. This position is often filled by someone in transition from Controller to VP Finance and usually goes by the title of Director of Finance.

The Five Key Components of the Finance/Accounting Function

There are five fundamental components of the finance/accounting function. The first three functions are common to Controllers, Directors and VPs of Finance. Operational input and the maximization of enterprise value are functions normally associated with the titles Director of Finance and Vice President of Finance.

Financial Accounting: The first function of any accounting department is the production of timely and accurate financial data. Out of this data comes the required financial reporting that is required by law and directed at outside stakeholders such as investors, banks and the various levels of government for tax remittance. Financial reports are historically accurate and can have a predictive value for people who are making financial decisions about the company.

Management Reporting: Management reporting is used primarily within the company and is tailored to assist management run and monitor the performance of the organization. Budget and forecasts, historical and anticipated raw material cost reports and new venture feasibility studies are all examples of management reporting.

Internal Controls: These are the internal policies and procedures that protect the company's assets. Internal controls define specific roles and responsibilities of employees with the intended outcome of preventing errors, theft, embezzlement, expense record inflation, etc.

Operational Input: While various members of the executive team such as the VP Sales or VP Operations may understand their particular discipline inside and out, they may not fully understand the financial and/or tax implications of their respective operations. Finance can and should work closely with management to support their operations and add value that would have otherwise gone unrealized.

Maximizing Enterprise Value: For most, if not all, owner-managers, their company represents the biggest investment they are ever likely to make. Whether their plan is to keep running the company until they leave feet first, pass it along to the next generation or eventually sell all or part of their enterprise to a third party, it's crucial that they keep an eye on enterprise value. A good financial executive can help the owner-manager maximize their company's enterprise value in the present day and assist them in realizing that value in the indefinite future, should they choose.

Straight Answers to Real Questions:

Falling Through the Expectation Gap

Question: My Controller recently resigned and I need to replace him. My first approach to finding a replacement was to post the job online. I didn't get much in the way of good candidates from my posting, but I did get a lot of calls and e-mails from recruiters assuring me that they had the perfect candidate on hand.

I sorted through my e-mails and picked three recruiters who seemed to specialize in accounting and finance and sent them all an e-mail with the job description and salary range. I listed my key criteria in terms of technical skills and industry experience and asked each of the recruiters to submit their one or two best candidates in the next few days.

The net result of this exercise was that I got resumés, but I didn't get good candidates. I wouldn't characterize any of the resumés as bad, but I wouldn't characterize any of them as good, either. They were about the same quality as what I got from the job-board posting I put up.

So, what's the deal here? These recruiters all assured me that they could fill my job and, when I finally give them a shot, they drop the ball. If they're so specialized in accounting, why didn't any of them produce the perfect candidate?

Answer: Even if the recruiters you reached out to are all specialists in the finance and accounting market with access to an in-house database of hundreds of resumés of readily available candidates, that's no guarantee that any of them will happen to know the right candidate for you at the time that you ask for them. For one thing, active candidates have a shelf life, especially at the more junior levels. Very good candidates don't tend to linger very long in a placement agency's database; they find jobs fairly quickly, either through the agency or on their own. Which means that the majority of candidates a recruiter can access quickly are what you saw – average.

That being said, it's possible or even probable that one of the recruiters did happen to know of someone who was perfect for your Controller role. But when approached on the job, that perfect someone wasn't interested in your job. Job seekers have a list of criteria as well – geography, industry, career path, etc., and just because they're a fit for you, it doesn't mean you're a fit for them.

If you really want to find strong candidates for your Controller role, you need to have a strategy that will access all the potential candidates who could fit your position, not just the active candidates that are a placement agency's stock in trade. Find a recruiter that's set up to do actual headhunting on your behalf, commit to find your candidate through that firm (and commit to paying them) and get comfortable with the fact that the process is going to take some time.

3

What to Look For/What to Look Out For

A Primer on Accounting Designations

The very first criterion you're probably going to put on your shopping list is that the successful candidate will need to have their CPA designation. However, what you may not be aware of is that the CPA designation is actually a new designation in Canada and comprises what were formerly Chartered Accountants (CAs), Certified Management Accountants (CMAs) and Certified General Accountants (CGAs).

Just to make it more confusing, the American system also produces CPAs. But in their case, CPA stands for Certified Public Accountant whereas the Canadian designation stands for Chartered Professional Accountant.

The Canadian CPA association is moving towards a standardized education/qualification process with all designated Canadian accountants unifying under the CPA banner. Until 2022, existing designated accountants will use their legacy designation in addition to the CPA designation: "CPA, CA," "CPA, CMA" or "CPA, CGA." Anyone earning their designation in or after 2016 will simply be a CPA. Historically, the CA, CMA and CGA designations had very different educational and qualification programs and understanding the nuances of each designation can be useful in choosing the right finance executive.

Generally speaking, the differentiating factors for each designation are as follows:

Chartered Accountant: The CA program focused on public company reporting and accounting, and most CA students article with public accounting firms. The Chartered Accountant training program traditionally has been considered to be the most rigorous of the three designations. Although well-grounded in all aspects of accounting, CAs tend to have better training in financial reporting, audit and tax. Because of the nature of articling at a public accounting firm, most CAs have had a well-rounded business education and have been exposed to a number of different companies and industries during their years in audit.

Certified Management Accountant: The CMA program focused on management accounting, but also provided a general education in financial accounting and tax. CMAs are less involved in the clerical aspects of accounting and more involved in management reporting, performance measurement and management. Because of their roots in the industrial sector, CMAs often have strong backgrounds in manufacturing issues such as costing and inventory.

Certified General Accountant: The CGA program took a general approach on education, allowing candidates to focus on their own financial career choices. CGAs are the utility players in accounting, able to fill multiple financial management needs within a business.

If you were to rate the three accounting designations in terms of degree of difficulty to obtain and technical rigour, CAs head the list, followed by CMAs, then CGAs.

In most instances, for owner-managers hiring at the Vice President of Finance level, the designation a prospective candidate started out with shouldn't make much of a difference. However, knowing the difference between the three designations can be useful in a couple of ways.

In terms of technical training, there are situations where one designation may be preferable to the others. For example, if you're contemplating going public someday, someone with the Chartered Accountant designation would probably be the better choice. Or, if you run a manufacturing concern and costing and inventory are important recurring issues, someone with a CMA designation may be preferred.

The other consideration to keep in mind is the past and projected career trajectory of a prospective CFO. Historically, Chartered Accountants enter the world of private industry on a higher rung of the career ladder and with higher pay than their CMA and CGA counterparts. The premium that CAs are able to command early in their careers can often still be in effect by the time you're interviewing them to be your next CFO.

You may find yourself interviewing a CA candidate with 10 years' experience who's asking for the same price tag as the CGA candidate with 20 years' experience. In cases like this, the CA will undoubtedly be on a steeper career trajectory than their CGA rival. If the CA and CGA candidates are equally up to the challenges your CFO job presents today, then the question becomes: "Who's the better hire for tomorrow?"

If you think your business will look very much the same in five years, hire the CGA. If you think the next five years will be characterized by rapid growth and unforeseen challenges and opportunities, the CA may be your better bet.

What to Look For

There's no "one size fits all" formula when it comes to hiring a CFO. But there are some traits and qualifications that you should be looking for when you're putting together your hiring criteria.

Industry Experience

The more senior a finance professional gets, the less they are defined by their accounting knowledge and the more they're defined by their industry knowledge. Bio-pharma, software, auto parts manufacturing and many other industry segments all have operational and accounting issues that are particular to their industry. For example, as much as someone from outside the auto parts manufacturing industry can in time figure those issues out, at the executive level it makes much more sense for an auto parts manufacturer to hire someone who's already had firsthand and extensive knowledge of whatever those issues happen to be. Not only will they get up to speed quickly, they may also be able to bring some fresh operational insights to the table.

Cross-Functional Experience

Expertise in accounting and finance should be a given for any CFO. However, the CFO can and should be able to function as a utility player and take charge of duties and projects that fall well outside of the world of finance and accounting. In most owner-managed businesses, the CFO also oversees human resources, IT, administration, facilities management as well as any special projects that happen to crop up.

Operational Orientation

A CFO who understands the organization at both the granular and macro levels is in a unique position to come up with strategic insights on how to improve operations. At a tactical level, the CFO can help other members of the executive team understand the real time operational and financial consequences of their decisions. The CFO can advise operational management on issues such as realizing cost and corporate efficiencies, systems changes, vendor selection, contemplated capital expenditures and new business initiatives.

Communication Skills

Sales executives may speak sales, logistics executives may speak logistics, manufacturing executives may speak manufacturing but finance executives need to be able to effectively speak to all of those line executives in their own language. If the CFO can't speak the language of the rest of the executive team, their ability to influence behaviours or add value to operations will be severely curtailed.

Strong Technical Network

Although the CFO position demands a very high level of expertise in any number of areas, no one knows everything, and financial executives should be willing to reach out to the appropriate experts to help out when necessary. When a CFO knows a range of technical and professional experts, it amplifies the scope and effectiveness of their position.

Credibility with Outside Stakeholders

In many ways, your CFO is the face of the company to your stakeholder community. This is the person that deals with the CRA, your bank, suppliers, major customers, auditors and shareholders. They need to have the ability to deal equally well with a wide range of stakeholders and present themselves in a positive, professional light. Above all, they need to be, and be perceived to be, competent with a high level of integrity.

Strategic Advisor

The top finance person in any company should be able to act as a trusted advisor to the CEO and the rest of the management team. The real added value that a CEO should be looking for in their CFO is the ability to help shape the strategic vision for the future of the business and implement and monitor the plans that will help realize that vision.

Future Potential

Whenever you contemplate hiring a CFO, whether it's a newly created position for your organization or replacing an incumbent, you should always think about filling not only the position you're recruiting for now, but also the position this will become in the future. If you own a company that has historically been growing slowly and you don't anticipate that to change, anyone you hire who does as good a job as your CFO in the short term will very likely still be doing a good job for you five or 10 years from now.

However, companies experiencing or antici- pating rapid growth need to ensure that the person they hire today has the ability to morph into the CFO they'll require in the future. If your company is currently earning $40 million in revenue and has been growing at a rate of 20% a year, don't hire for what you are today, hire for what you're going to be three to five years from now. At a year-over-year

20% rate of growth, your company will be a $100-million business five years from now. You should hire someone who can help you achieve that milestone and who has the skill set and aptitude to be comfortable as the CFO of a company of that size.

What to Look Out For

Avoid Reflexive Recruiting

When you have an opening for a financial executive, you can look at filling that position in one of two ways. The most common approach is to replace the person who's leaving. The better approach is to fill the position that's open. They may sound like the same thing, but they're not.

When you have to replace your Vice President of Finance or your Controller, and they've been in the position a long time, you have an opportunity to maximize the value that particular position could bring to the organization. As much as you might like the incumbent, and as much as they may have done a great job for you over the years, the position you need to fill today is often not the same position you hired for way back when. In fact, as much as the incumbent may have been a valued member of the management team for the past number of years, it's entirely possible that your company and the position have outgrown that person and you should be looking for an entirely different profile when you go to replace them.

Replacing your current incumbent is an opportunity to reengineer the CFO role and properly align the position with the business's current and anticipated future demands. If your company has grown significantly since you last had to hire your top finance person, you will probably find that the role has changed significantly, and you'll also find that what the market has to offer you in terms of candidates has changed significantly as well.

As your company grows in size and sophistication, your CFO position becomes much more attractive to a better qualified, more sophisticated candidate pool. And you won't necessarily have to pay a large premium to attract those candidates.

What usually happens is that over the course of their tenure with the company, the incumbent will have received year-over-year salary increases. Even if those increases have been relatively small, they tend to act like compound interest and the net effect is that the incumbent's compensation will usually keep pace with the general market even if their skill set does not. If you're paying your current CFO $180,000 a year (plus bonus), you can probably replace them with someone with a lot more horsepower for about the same level of compensation. Even if you end up having to pay a 10% premium over what you paid the previous incumbent, you may find that you'll get 50% or even 100% more value from your new CFO.

Avoid Buying On Sale

If you post a job on LinkedIn or put the word out to your network that you're looking for a CFO, many of the people that respond to you will be unemployed. And many of those people will have been unemployed for quite some time.

And because they've been on the street for a while, you may end up interviewing someone who was previously in a more senior position than the one you have on offer. However, inasmuch as that candidate was used to a bigger job with bigger pay, they may make a very strong case on why they'd be willing to take your job at the pay that you're offering. (A variation on this theme is the unemployed candidate who lives in a distant suburb who swears that they won't mind the 75-minute commute into your part of town.

In most cases, the candidate is sincere in their argument. They honestly believe that they'll be happy in your job, at that location, for that pay, in the years to come. However, bear in mind that the candidate's decision-making process may have been influenced by any number of factors, including lack of cash flow, loss of self-confidence or boredom. Being unemployed is no walk in the park for anyone, and the longer someone is unemployed, the less fussy about their future employment they become.

If you do decide to hire one of these candidates at what is essentially a fire-sale price, there's a real possibility of flight risk. Not right away and probably not in the first year or so. But once your new CFO has gotten their legs under them in their new job and have re-established their cash flow, self-esteem and professional engagement, they may begin to view their current employment in a new light.

Most will not actively be on the market for a new position for at least a couple of years, but they will often be susceptible to calls from headhunters or people in their network who refer them to new gigs. They'll usually respond to these opportunities reluctantly, but if they're offered a position more in line with their previous level of responsibility and compensation, it will be very hard for them to turn that down.

Every hiring situation is unique and there are any number of exceptions to what I've described above. For example, if a financial executive antici-pates that they will want to retire in the next 10 years or so, they may happily settle in to a job less challenging than what they've been accustomed to. Or perhaps, the job and compensation you have on offer is less than what they had before, but by virtue of your anticipated growth, the CFO can reasonably expect to make up any lost ground and, indeed, end up ahead of the challenge/compensation curve. But unless the reason the ostensibly overqualified candidate wants to take your job makes a lot of sense, you should think twice before signing on the dotted line.

Straight Answers to Real Questions:

The Terminator

Question: I own and manage a $45-million owner-managed industrial tool manufacturer out in Mississauga. Our company is family owned and my three brothers are all involved in the business. Our dad started the business 40 years ago, and although he's "retired" now, he still takes an active interest in what's going on.

Our Vice President of Finance resigned a few months ago and I'm having a heck of time trying to replace him. It's not that I haven't interviewed some good prospects; I've been working with an executive search firm and they've been showing me good people. On three separate occasions I've taken someone through the entire interview process only to have that candidate vetoed by one of my brothers. It's actually the same brother doing the vetoing each time and he won't tell me why he's nixed each candidate, except that he "didn't get a good feeling about them."

Not only is this making me a little nuts, sooner or later not having a CFO in place is going to have some negative repercussions on the business. Any suggestions?

Answer: Rule number one when you're hiring anyone for your executive team is to ensure that every stakeholder participates in and signs off on the candidate profile before the search starts. Even if one of the stakeholders protests that they don't have anything to contribute to the process, they still need to be a part of the discussion so that they know exactly how the inputs resulted in the preferred candidate profile.

Discuss how much experience, what kind of technical expertise and what personality/leadership traits you're going to be looking for. Make sure everyone at the table will be able to recognize the right candidate when they walk through the door. If there's any quibbling or conflicting opinions, do your best to get them resolved at this stage.

This exercise should go a long way to prevent the kind of frustration you're experiencing now. If you haven't already done so, I would get your dad and your brothers in a room and have this conversation.

Of course, your brother who keeps vetoing the candidates may just be being ornery for the sake of it or he may be engaging in some sort of fraternal power struggle with you. In which case, the best recourse is to tactfully recommend to your dad and your siblings that since you've been unable to crack this particular nut that they should take on the challenge of recruiting the new CFO. More specifically, you should recommend that your brother with the veto take the lead on this.

Everybody has an opinion about how you should be digging the ditch until you hand them a shovel. I think you'll find that your recalcitrant sibling will quickly hand the shovel back to you and finally let you get the job done.

4

Compensation Considerations

The Challenge of Benchmarking CFO Compensation

When it comes to benchmarking compensation, big companies have it relatively easy. They've got human resources departments, access to compensation consultants like Mercer and the best built-in tool available for compensation benchmarking: ongoing turnover.

Large companies that experience ongoing turnover get periodic, market-based information on what skill sets and/or levels of experience are worth. If inflation has crept in because of a booming economy or a lack of a particular skill set, companies see it as it occurs and can gradually adjust their pay scales accordingly. If there's a glut on the market, companies may cut wages but, more typically, they'll hire better for the same dollars.

Owner-managed businesses don't (or shouldn't) experience the same kind of turnover and may not need to go to the market for years at a time. So when they do need to recruit someone from the outside to fill an executive position like Vice President of Finance, they often don't know what they need to pay.

The default position is to use the outgoing incumbent's remuneration as the set point. However, if the company hasn't hired for a number of years, there are three factors that can make this the wrong approach: (1) they may need to hire a different profile; (2) they may not have kept up to the market in terms of management/executive compensation; or (3) the incumbent's salary may have been steadily rising over the past number of years but their relative value to the company hasn't.

Owner-managers who want to benchmark CFO compensation will often turn to one of the salary surveys published by the big recruitment firms. I took a look at one of these surveys recently and it reported that for companies with revenues of $50 million to $100 million, the salary range for Vice Presidents of Finance was between $121,750 and $164,000.

Somewhat confusedly, the same survey reported that companies of that size paid their CFOs in a range of $131,250 to $177,750 (in companies with revenues between $50 million and $100 million, the CFO and VP Finance are always paid the same).

If I were the CEO of a $75-million manufacturer and I needed to hire for the top financial spot in my organization, I don't think I would find that information all that useful. There's a 36% differential between the reported low and the reported high end of the range – how do I decide where to peg my particular CFO's salary?

That's the problem with most salary surveys – the ranges they quote are too broad to be of any real use to an employer trying to benchmark compensation. In surveys like this, the data is usually taken from all the placements that the firm made in that reporting period. The main problem with this approach is that the people being placed and the firms doing the hiring are going to cover a very wide spectrum of variables.

For instance, if you own a manufacturing company in a mature market with no growth plans and tight margins, you may hire a VP Finance for what is basically a maintenance-type function at a salary of $140,000 and a 10% bonus potential. However, if you own a software services company that has been enjoying dramatic growth and you anticipate that you'll stay on the current trajectory, you may pay your CFO $225,000 plus a bonus worth up to 30% of salary.

Which brings me to the other issue with salary surveys of this sort – they only reflect the salaries for candidates that the recruitment firm's clients happened to have hired. This data usually does not reflect actual market rates. The range cited in the survey I looked at suggests that $177,750 is the top end of CFO salaries for companies with $50 to $100 million in revenue, which is definitely not the case – they're actually quite a bit higher.

It may not be scientific, but the best way to benchmark compensation for your Vice President of Finance or any other management/executive position in your team is anecdotal. Talk to your fellow CEOs in the same industries and specialist executive recruiters to get a general idea of what you need to pay to attract the calibre of CFO that you need.

Once you actually get into the search, you'll have an opportunity to window shop. Generally speaking, financial executives get paid fairly. If you took a sample of 10 Directors of Finance working in $25-million manufacturing companies competing in a mature market, most if not all of those people would be on the same career trajectory and would all be earning a similar amount. If you took a sample of 10 VPs of Finance working in growth-oriented high-tech firms, their career trajectories and pay packages would be very similar as well.

You'll know if you've pegged your compensation package correctly once your search is underway and producing candidates. If you see a few good candidates currently working in companies analogous to yours in terms of size and complexity, they will either affirm that your initial compensation range is appropriate or cause you to adjust it to the fair market rate.

Putting Together the Overall Package

Hiring a CFO who will advance your company's agenda and business objectives requires strategic thinking on a number of fronts, not least of which is compensation. Not only will a well-thought-out compensation plan bring the best candidate to the table, it will align your CFO properly with your company's interests. This is especially true for owner-managed companies where the CFO can have a significant impact on the overall success of the business. When structuring your CFO's compensation plan, your main considerations should include the following:

Base Salary: Your overall compensation plan should reflect the size, complexity and growth pattern of your company. Since the base salary is the most visible (and usually the biggest) component of that plan, this is the first thing private company CFOs look at when they're contemplating a new position. Once you have a benchmark number (as discussed above), tailor it to your particular operation. There a few factors that come into play here. Location (i.e., Toronto pays more than Hamilton), industry, company growth trajectory, etc. – all have an effect on where you set the bar.

It's important to get this number right. If you go to the market with a number that's too low, some great candidates will take a pass, even if the variable pay component of your compensation plan offers real upside potential.

Short-Term Incentives: Short-term incentives usually take the form of annual bonuses and are designed to focus the CFO's attention on achieving specific project and activity goals that will help you and your company achieve your near-term business objectives. These goals should be explicitly stated and performance metrics negotiated and agreed upon up front. Examples of these goals could include:

- *Improving profit margins by a specific value*

- *Successfully leading an ERP implementation*

- *Securing new financing arrangements*

- *Quarterbacking a new facilities build-out*

This is usually a cash bonus and is calculated as a percentage of the CFO's annual salary.

Long-Term Incentives: One way to maximize your CFO's overall contribution and to motivate them to increase enterprise value over the long run is to offer some form of long-term incentive. By definition, the performance period for a long-term incentive typically runs between three and five years, with the executive not receiving any pay from the incentive until the end of the performance period.

Public companies have a real advantage over private companies in attracting and retaining key executives through the granting of stock options. However, private companies can also achieve that end through a grant of restricted stock or a cash based long-term incentive plan that mirrors the payout under an equity-based plan. While not an option for most private companies, in certain circumstances it may be a key component in attracting the right CFO.

Straight Answers to Real Questions:

There Will Be Blood

Question: I recently decided to expand my footprint in my particular market by buying a company whose product line complements mine. I plan to keep them as a separate entity and need to make some operational and personnel changes to get the company up to our standard. There's a lot of streamlining to be done, and I'm going to have to get rid of a lot of driftwood at all levels and bring in some fresh blood to get this place on the right track.

The purge is going to start at the executive suite and will continue right down through the ranks. I'm going to need some help recruiting and plan on engaging some recruitment firms. I know that some firms work on a contingency fee basis and some firms work on a retained fee basis. Who do I use for what?

Answer: For your "plug and play" roles, contingency firms are your best bet. Placement agencies that specialize in junior level positions should have a ready stock of tested, qualified candidates at hand. I recommend that you only work with one firm at a time and give them a week or two to really give it their best effort to fill your position. If you don't get what you're looking for from the first firm you decide to deal with, open it up to some other firms.

For positions at the executive level, you should work with a retained firm that has experience in whatever function you're recruiting for. Some placement agencies will have some executive level candidates on file, but this kind of search requires a recruiter to go beyond who they know today and conduct a thorough search of the market. In addition, senior level searches require a much higher degree of technical sophistication to properly assess potential candidates.

Beware of placement agencies that purport to be executive search firms. As much as they may protest that they will do a thorough job for you, if they work primarily on a contingency-fee basis, they're a placement agency. Which means that they're in the business of placing the people they have on hand; they are not in the business of conducting an executive search.

5

DIY Recruiting

Quantity of Choice = Quality of Decision

I'll confess right from the outset that I'm not a fan of do-it-yourself recruiting. I'm not just talking my own book; I've been a recruiter for a lot of years and if there's one thing I know, it's that the quality of the hiring authority's decision is a direct function of the quality of the short list they interview, which is a function of the number of candidates canvassed. If you use an executive recruiter (preferably me) to recruit your next CFO, you will be accessing a very large number of candidates who could be a good fit for your position. If you decide to do-it-yourself, you'll only access a very small percentage of the candidate pool available to you.

But if you do decide to DIY the recruitment process, you have three basic avenues you can

explore: networking, posting the job online and
direct recruiting on LinkedIn.

Networking

The first person you should reach out to is the
partner you deal with at your public accounting
firm. Partners in public accounting are nonpareil
networkers and will inevitably know one or two
senior financial executives who are looking for a
new home. You may also ask your banker or lawyer
for referrals. Professionals who deal with owner-
managers are often approached by unemployed
executives looking to be referred. You can also tap
into the various networking groups catering to
finance executives such as The Finance Network or
HAPPEN. Their memberships are usually comprised
of people actively looking for new positions.

Job Boards

Caveat Emptor

As much as job boards are the most popular option
for companies on the market for new talent, they
aren't nearly as effective a recruiting tool as most
people think. There's no question that job postings result in receiving a lot of resumés. But hiring
authorities shouldn't assume that just because
they've received 50 or 75 responses to their posting
that a fair number of them are going to be a good fit.

The number of responses to a job posting can be misleading. Job boards are the number one resource for active job hunters, many of whom are unemployed. Since it costs nothing to respond to a posting, people tend to respond to anything and everything that may be in their particular ball park. So even though the hiring authority may receive 75 resumés, most of them will be on a spectrum ranging from kinda/sorta qualified to not-at-all qualified. Only a relatively few resumés will actually be in the ballpark the posting was hoping to attract.

Fit the Candidate to the Job, Not the Job to the Candidate

The key to success in posting jobs online is to have a very clear idea of what the ideal candidate will look like before you start reviewing resumés. Be very specific about the key criteria necessary for success in the job. If you have a clear and firm idea of what you're looking for before you post the job, you'll avoid the trap many people fall in to – modifying the job to fit the available candidate(s).

This is a definite hazard when you're relying on job boards to produce your candidate pool. You assume that your ad response represents a fair cross section of the candidates available to you, and if none of them fit your job, you may decide that you need to change your requirements or expectations to accommodate the people you're interviewing.

But since job boards only give you access to candidates that are actively on the market, the response you get doesn't represent a fair cross section of the candidates actually available. It's entirely possible that you'll get no qualified responses at all to your posting. In which case, don't change your criteria to suit the candidates, keep looking for the candidates that suit your criteria.

An Informal Survey of LinkedIn Job-Posting Responses

I recently reviewed a number of senior postings we had on LinkedIn over a one-year period. The jobs posted were either CFO, VP Finance or Director of Finance. I reviewed all the responses and totalled up the number of respondents and the number of those people who actually made it onto a short list. The highest number of respondents on a single posting was 168; the lowest was 52. The average number of respondents on a posting was 87.4.

The average success rate in terms of qualified candidates, people that ended up on my short list, was 1.14%. For every 87.4 resumés that I reviewed in response to my job postings, only one of them would have made it to an interview with my client.

Out of all of the postings I reviewed, it worked out that LinkedIn applicants produced 17.5% of the candidates I presented on my short lists and 14.3% of the people hired by my clients over this period.

Linking IN

LinkedIn has two main avenues available to you to source candidates. The first and most obvious recruitment tool available is the job-posting feature, which we've just discussed. Postings are relatively inexpensive and are good for a period of 30 days. Job postings will capture the active candidates who have up-to-date resumés, time to actively pursue opportunities and no issues with confidentiality.

The other way to use LinkedIn as a recruiting tool is to run searches yourself (or have human resources do it) and send InMails to the people you think may be a good candidate for your position. Just be aware that unless you have the very expensive LinkedIn Recruiter licence, this approach will only give you access to the people that are within one or two degrees of your own (or HR's) LinkedIn network, and the number of search filters available is quite limited.

This approach will let you target some of the "passive" candidate pool of people who might be willing to entertain other opportunities but are not actively on the market. This approach is a bit analogous to a direct mail campaign – you have no idea if the people you're sending InMails to are on the market or not. But if you send out enough InMails, you will get some positive responses, and some of those people may turn out to be viable candidates for your job.

Are Some Candidates Enough Candidates?

There's no question that networking, job boards and social media will net you some candidates. You may end up hiring someone from your DIY efforts, but the odds are against you hiring the best possible candidate. You'll end up hiring the best of that particular pool of candidates. You'll be overlooking about 85% of the other candidates that could and should be available to you.

This approach may work out for you if you're going to be satisfied with someone who ends up being an adequate hire. However, in my 30 years of recruiting financial executives, I've yet to have a CEO give me a mandate to find them an adequate CFO. They all want a great CFO, and that's not something you should be willing to leave to chance.

If you want to play the odds and try to avoid the time and expense of a full-blown search, by all means give the do-it-yourself option a shot. But before you do, have a clear idea of what the ideal candidate looks like and don't settle for less. If you don't see what you're looking for, it doesn't mean they're not out there; it just means that you're going to have to hire someone to go looking for them.

Straight Answers to Real Questions:

► Let the Right One In

Question: I own a specialty retail chain with stores across Canada. I haven't had occasion to hire for a few years but recently our Controller quit and we need to replace her.

I'm actually pretty happy with how the search has been going. We're getting a decent response from our online posting, we've had a number of internal referrals and my professional network has produced a few good candidates as well.

My problem is I don't know how to separate the really good candidates from the pretty good candidates; all of the candidates I've been interviewing seem awfully similar to me. They all have their CPA, work in retail, are fairly personable and articulate, and they all know their way around a spreadsheet.

How I do I know which one of these candidates will turn out to be the best fit for the job?

Answer: Since you mentioned that all of the candidates are articulate and personable, I'm going to have to assume that you like all of them equally in terms of a personality fit. And since they all seem to have the sort of experience and technical chops you're looking for, it looks like they'll all be able to competently perform the job you have on offer.

So that leaves you with one criterion that you can use to tease out who's going to be the best candidate for the job – potential. Every time you hire someone, you should be looking beyond the job you're hiring for and take into consideration what the next job for the person might be and the probable time frame before that person is ready for that next job.

If you're looking for someone to be your Controller for the next five-plus years, then the best candidate for that job won't be the brightest, most ambitious person on your short list. Conversely, if you have big growth plans for your company and you can see your Controller role morphing into a VP Finance position in the foreseeable future, the obvious high-flyer will be your best choice.

6

Working with Recruiters

In the early days of the recruitment industry (which wasn't all that long ago), it was easy to distinguish between the two very distinct types of recruitment firms – placement agencies and executive search firms. Placement agencies were used for hiring junior and clerical staff, and executive search firms were retained to recruit executives.

As the world of business became more sophisticated and specialized, so did the service offerings of placement agencies. In addition to providing junior staff, placement agencies began to recruit for highly specialized technical professionals such as engineers, accountants and IT specialists.

As placement agencies have been migrating up into the more senior markets, the terms they use to describe their service offerings borrow heavily from the world of the executive search firms. But the placement agency industry runs on an entirely different business model than the executive search industry, and the economic drivers of their model dictate that they can't actually offer a true executive search, regardless of what their marketing materials might suggest.

Placement Agencies

The value proposition of placement agencies is that they have qualified applicants that are immediately available for interviewing. They make extensive use of job postings and networking sites to acquire their stock and are constantly triaging and assessing applicants to ensure that they have an adequate supply of ready product. The applicants they represent are usually very active in the market, so agencies need to aggressively market their services to ensure that they have a constant stream of orders to match their applicants. Since placement agencies work on a contingency-fee basis (usually non-exclusive), they can't afford to spend too much time or effort on any one assignment. Most placement agencies make efforts to ensure a good fit, but they are limited by the applicant pool available to them at that time and the pressure to get resumés to the client quickly.

Even if you opt to work with one placement agency on an exclusive, contingency-fee basis, that's still not a guarantee that you'll get the results you're looking for. Your recruiter will make the extra effort to tap into the agency's database, do research on sites like LinkedIn and will do some actual headhunting on your behalf. But since there's still no guarantee of payment, there are limits to how long and how hard your recruiter will be willing to work on your assignment.

Placement agencies are fine when it comes to hiring junior and mid-level staff. However, for the most part, choosing a placement agency to recruit your CFO is not a good idea. This is not a reflection on any particular placement agency; it's just that the agency business model does not lend itself to doing the kind of search required to guarantee a successful hire.

Executive Search Firms

The value proposition of executive search firms is that they have sophisticated research and recruitment capabilities that allow them to conduct searches across the country or around the world. The high-end executive search is a high-cost, high-service, low-volume business. Their fees are based on 30% to 35% of total remuneration with add-ons and charge backs that can take the overall fee to over 40%. Executive search firms spend considerable time and effort to acquire their clients, and they work very hard to keep these clients happy. Executive recruiters are usually very experienced professionals, and the focus of their efforts lies in making sure that their research and recruiting result in the best executive and cultural fit for their client. Since search firms are always paid (and paid very well), they focus on quality of results, not volume of work.

In theory, when a company retains an executive search firm, it should reasonably expect close to a 100% success rate since it is paying the full bill. However, various industry studies put the success ratio of fully retained executive search firms at closer to 70%, suggesting that not all executive search firms are created equal and that selecting the right firm is critically important.

Companies should be wary of executive search firms that claim to be able to recruit for middle-market CFO assignments. Executive search firms may claim that they treat every client and assignment the same way, but the business model of national and multinational executive recruiters drives them towards big-ticket searches that pay enough to justify the time and effort required to properly execute on them. Not only do searches in the middle market generate much smaller fees, they can also take more effort than senior searches simply because there are more possible candidates to survey.

How You Pay Determines How You Play

Executive search firm versus placement agency is simply a choice between business models. Neither one is inherently "better" than the other; they each serve different parts of the market. A company's success with an outside recruiter, whether a placement agency or an executive search firm, isn't just a function of choosing the right firm to work with. Success in using an outside recruiter is also a function of using the right *kind* of firm for a company's recruitment needs. The key to working with outside recruiters is to remember that how they get paid determines how they actually work and what you should realistically expect from them.

Straight Answers to Real Questions:

▶ DIY Reference Checking

Question: I've been recruiting for a new CFO for my firm and I think we're just about ready to pull the trigger on someone. Before we make an offer to our finalist candidate, I'd like to check references. Should I ask the recruitment firm I'm working with to conduct the reference checks or should I hire an independent service?

Answer: Most professionals with a straightforward career history tend to have straightforward references – you'll hear what you're expecting to hear and it's usually fine to have the recruiter or other third party conduct the reference check. However, if your finalist candidate has hit a career speed bump in their recent past, you should be conducting that particular reference check yourself.

One of the problems with third-party reference checks is that they tend to pose stock questions and then faithfully record what are often stock answers. Employers are usually very reluctant to give bad references and will tend to gloss over problem areas and accentuate the positives of their previous employee.

A good reference check is characterized by challenging stock answers and digging deeper into nuanced or hedged responses. If there's an issue with the candidate that the reference has been skating around, enough pointed questions will eventually reveal the whole story, at least from the previous employer's point of view.

Your recruiter isn't really motivated to dig hard to get to the real story, and the third-party reference checker is usually working from a boilerplate question template. You have the most to lose if you hire the wrong person, so you should make it your policy to be just a little bit paranoid when it comes to reference checks and do them yourself when warranted.

7

The Interview Process

Before You Start

In order to be successful in hiring your next CFO, you need to be disciplined and rigorous about how you apply your filters throughout the process.

Your preferred candidate profile will have some "must-have" criteria and some "would-be-nice" criteria. You can apply the latter in the final stages of the search, but you must be strict on your "must-have" criteria at every stage of the search.

Before you start interviewing candidates, before you even start looking at the responses to your job postings or the resumés you get from your recruiter, visualize what your next CFO looks like. Are you looking for a very seasoned executive or are you looking for someone who still has lots of room to grow? If your company is operating in a mature market and there isn't a lot of room for growth, someone in the latter stages of their career who wants a home for the next 10 years may be a great candidate. If your business is growing like a weed and you anticipate that growth to continue, someone in the earlier stages of their career with lots of potential and runway ahead of them would probably be the better choice.

Once you've got a general idea of what your CFO should look like, get specific on your tangible (technical expertise, industry experience, etc.) and intangible (personality, management style, etc.) criteria.

Your technical criteria are going to be a function of your operations, current issues and anticipated threats and opportunities.

In terms of personality and cultural fit, the best yardstick is your current management team. Executives who've successfully worked together for some time tend to have a number of traits in common. Identify and articulate those traits and visualize how those traits might manifest in the people that you're going to interview.

Sorting Through Potential Candidates

After you've put together a detailed profile of the preferred candidate, it's time to start sorting through potential candidates.

If you're working with an outside recruiter, they should be taking care of the first stages of the selection process and only showing you the candidates that have successfully made their way through all of your filters and meet the key criteria you've specified.

However, if you're selecting from ad responses and referrals from your network yourself, your objective is to take the 85 or so applicants and narrow them down to three or four (hopefully) decent candidates.

As I discussed in Chapter 5, don't assume that just because someone has applied to your posting or has been referred to you that there's a good reason for you to consider them. It costs nothing for someone to throw their hat into the ring and as a result many unemployed people throw their hats into as many rings as they can find.

You can do a first pass of your ad responses by applying some basic filters to weed out the obvious non-starters. Factors such as wrong industry, bad track record, no designation, too senior or too junior will probably chop your field of candidates down by about 85% right off the top, which will leave you a dozen or so applicants to take a second look at.

Next, take a closer look at their resumés. You're not looking for technical criteria just yet – you just want to get a sense of who they are. If someone's resumé is very well written – good visual presentation, not too long or short, logical, history of successive responsibility and achievement, etc. – that person is worth another look. If the resumé is poorly written, has spelling or grammatical mistakes, is too long, has a recitation of bullet points in lieu of a story, etc. – you can safely put that resumé in the reject pile.

Of the applicants remaining, take a careful read of their resumés for your original critical criteria. Some of your must-have criteria will be obvious in the resumés (ERP implementations for example) and some won't be – you'll have to infer those from the resumé and confirm them in the interview.

The Interview

When you started the recruitment process, you put a lot of thought into what you wanted to accomplish by hiring for this position. You identified the key issues, threats and opportunities your new CFO would be addressing, and you have a good idea of the challenges your business and your CFO will be facing in the years to come. When you put together the variable pay component of your compensation plan for this position, you identified the key metrics with which you'd be judging the success of your new CFO.

These issues, opportunities and metrics should inform how you conduct the interview. You're looking for a way to allow the candidates to specifically show off their expertise and experience that directly address your key criteria and that give you an idea of how they think.

Before you get into the real meat and potatoes of the interview, I recommend that you first get a sense of the candidate's career path to date. Specifically, you want to know why they've made each move in their career. You're looking for consistency in their career choices and you're also trying to discover any career speed bumps they may have encountered along the way. Ideally, the candidate has moved up a ladder of successive challenges and accomplishments in a relatively straight line.

After you've got a sense of the candidate's career history and trajectory, it's time to get down to specifics. I recommend that you come to the next phase of the interview with a set of questions that will tease out the candidates' knowledge of, and experience with, the issues particular to your business and what you want this role to accomplish.

Besides having a set of questions on hand, it's also useful to have a couple of scenarios that you can lay out for the candidate and have them explain in detail how they would approach those particular situations. The scenarios you put forward could be situations that happened in your business that either turned out particularly well or particularly badly. These scenarios are instructive because you'll already know what the right approach was and what the wrong approach was. It will be illuminating to see how in line the candidate's thinking is with yours on the scenario that worked out well for you and what alternative solutions they may propose for the circumstance that turned out badly.

Structure your questions in such a way that they require full-narrative answers. Instead of "Do you have experience with ERP implementations?" ask "Take me through your toughest ERP implementation and explain your thought process and actions from vendor selection through to post implementation testing." Or, "How would you rate the success of that implementation and, in hindsight, what would you have done differently?"

Other questions you might ask could include:

"What key strategic initiatives have you worked on?"

"What was the extent of your interaction with operational management in your last position?"

"What was the toughest challenge that you and the rest of the management team of your last employer faced and how did you and the team meet that challenge?"

"How is the finance team and function in your current employer different from when you joined the firm?"

"What part do you play in the strategic planning process at your firm?"

"What was the toughest finance challenge you faced in the past five years and how did you address it?"

"What's your approach to maximizing enterprise value?" or "What have you done in your previous positions that materially improved enterprise value?"

"What's your approach to developing your team, and how do you deal with succession planning in the finance group?" or "If you got hit by a bus tomorrow, how well would your finance team function in your absence?"

These types of questions will give you a good idea of the range of skills the candidate brings to the table, their overall approach to problem solving and their management style.

Along with the questions that directly address any outstanding issues or projects you may have in mind, at some point you'll also need to address the "table stakes" knowledge and experience. You want to know that the candidate is fully quali-fied and competent in all the routine parts of the CFO's position. They include accounting knowl-edge, experience dealing with insurance matters, internal controls, banking and financing, financial and management reporting, budgets and forecasts, information technology, strategic planning and tax.

Unless you are uncommonly familiar with accounting, I recommend that at some point you have your public accounting firm partner get involved in the interview process and specifically drill down into the candidate's accounting knowledge.

The Interview Cycle

Generally speaking, I recommend that owner-managed companies put candidates through at least three tiers of interviews.

You should have four or five solid candidates in your first interview tier. These candidates should all have resumés with the requisite experience and skill sets and be at the right age and stage for your position. Everyone should be at least a pretty good fit going into the interview – your goal is to identify the candidate(s) who's the best fit of that lot.

If you start with a good short list, you should find that you're able to identify at least one person whom you feel is a very strong candidate for the job. If you conclude all four or five interviews and haven't identified someone you feel very positively about, don't settle – keep looking until you are confident that you have found someone who fits the bill.

Once you've settled on one or two very strong candidates, invite them back to meet with key members of your executive team. This could also include your public accounting partner and, if you have an advisory board, someone from there as well. This is a very important step, as not only does it give your team a chance to assess and give feedback on the candidate(s), it also gives the candidate a much better feel for your corporate culture.

The last interview should be a frank discussion between you and the candidate about what your expectations are and what the metrics for success for the job will be. Any questions or concerns from both sides should be addressed, and you and the candidate should be entirely comfortable with each other by the end of the conversation.

I recommend that the discussion around compensation start fairly early in the process. Prospective candidates will know your general compensation range when they start the process, and you will find out what their current compensation looks like during the first interview. As a candidate progresses through the interview process, you should start getting specific around their expectations and what a prospective package from you might look like. By the time you get to the offer stage, you and the finalist candidate should be very close to an agreement (at least tacitly) on what their prospective compensation would look like.

And by the time you get down the last stage of the interview process, no matter what your other criteria, you should have a very strong sense that you'll be able to establish a high degree of trust and rapport with this person. Some owner-managers set the bar too low on this particular criterion. In order for the CFO to make a material and positive impact on your company, you need to feel comfortable with consulting them on virtually all aspects of your business. And to the extent that you need to trust them, they need to trust you enough to challenge you when necessary and come up with ideas and initiatives that will help you further your plans for your business.

Straight Answers to Real Questions:

► Choosing Pain Over Suffering

Question: I hired a new Director of Finance about a year ago. The person we brought on board seemed fine in the first couple of months, but now I'm having some doubts. He did seem to be a bit on the quiet side when I interviewed him, but I just thought that was fairly standard with accountants. My problem with this guy is that he never seems to venture out his office. I see him at our management meetings, but other than that, he's kind of a phantom around here. My VP Sales and Director of Manufacturing tell me that he never comes to them to ask about their particular operations. To be fair, he and his team do produce management reports, but he doesn't take the time or trouble to sit down with the individual members of the executive team and really drill down into what the implications of those reports are.

I've talked to him about my concerns, but it doesn't seem to be making much of an impact. Do you have any ideas on how to get him more engaged in adding value to operations?

Answer: It sounds to me like you're in the classic management conundrum of having to choose between pain and suffering. If you've talked to this guy and he isn't making a sincere and obvious effort to conform to your expectations, there's no reason to believe that he'll ever be the Director of Finance you need him to be.

There could be any number of reasons he hides in his office – he could be shy, more comfortable with spreadsheets than people, bogged down in minutia, etc. But whatever the reason, it just doesn't matter – he's not performing to spec.

Basically, your choice is to put up with this guy and hope for small, incremental improvements and then fire him two years from now when you've finally suffered enough, or you could start the painful process of replacing him right now.

My advice is to do yourself a favour and opt for the pain option right away. You're going to get there someday anyway and you might as well forgo the one or two years of suffering.

8

Steering Around the Potholes on the Road to Success

The process of recruiting a member of the executive team is not as straightforward as most other business endeavours. Even after all the tangibles have been addressed, like education, technical qualifications and industry experience, there are still the intangibles like personality and cultural fit to figure out.

It's common for owner-managers to run into some speed bumps when recruiting for a CFO. These speed bumps don't usually cause a search to go off the rails; typically, they just add extra time and expense to the process. However, there are a number of potholes that owner-managers commonly fall into that usually result in an average hire and all too often a bad hire.

Pothole #1:

A Muddled Mandate

Owner-managers often have a sales, engineering or operations background and, although they're usually functionally fluent in financial matters, they often don't know what they could and should be asking from the CFO function. This is especially true when they're going to the market for a CFO for the first time. Of course, they know they want the accounting function to run smoothly, but beyond that, they may not have defined the specifics that will spell success in the position.

Unless a hiring authority knows exactly what they need, it's very hard to parse the candidates they're looking at and decide who would be the best person for the job. A lack of hard and fast criteria with which to judge the candidate pool often leads to the hiring authority relying solely on gut instinct to make the final decision. While this doesn't necessarily result in a bad hire, it usually doesn't result in a very good hire either.

Pothole #2:

Fitting the Job to the Candidate

Networking and job boards are the most popular venues for sourcing candidates for most owner-managers. And although networking and job boards may produce a *good number of candidates*, they don't usually produce *a number of good candidates*. So, what often happens is the owner-manager ends up meeting a number of people who meet some of their key criteria, but none of the candidates meet all of their key criteria.

In this scenario, what can happen is the hiring authority builds up the aspects of the position that play to a candidate's strengths and either minimizes or deals off the parts of the job that the candidate is weak in.

If you're not getting your must-haves in your current tranche of candidates, don't let expediency compel you to make the wrong hire. Sticking it out until you get what you were originally looking for, or even starting the search over, is a much more economical approach in terms of time and money than hiring the wrong person now and replacing them with the right person later.

Pothole #3:

Hiring for Who You Wish You Were, Not Who You Are

As Polonius advises his son Laertes: "To thine own self be true." Translated into recruitment terms: "Hire for who you are, not who you wish to be."

Some industries, some businesses and some owner-managers are more demanding than others. If you or your business happen to fall into that category, it's important that you recognize it and make that part of your search profile. You want to get to know your prospective CFO well, warts and all, before you hire them. You want them to know you just as well, with whatever warts you happen to have, before they sign on the dotted line.

If 60-hour weeks have been the norm for the past few years, then that's part of the culture and it's not going to change anytime soon. If your company has fallen on hard times and part of the CFO's job will be to stave off anxious creditors, make sure prospective candidates know that up front. If you like to have the final say in all decisions, acknowledge that as well. Whatever the company culture, your management style or particular challenges of the position might be, you need to recognize them up front, be prepared to articulate them openly and honestly, and factor them into the recruitment strategy. It may take a little longer to fill the position, but in the end the position will be filled by the right candidate and that will save you a lot of grief and expense down the road.

Pothole #4:

Not Working the Numbers

I've made this point a number of times already in previous chapters, but I cannot stress this enough: consistently and reliably hiring well for a CFO position is a matter of working the numbers. And for the numbers to work well, they need to be large numbers. Referrals and job boards will only generate a small fraction (about 15%) of the potential candidates that may be available to you. The key to consistent, successful recruitment is canvassing a large number of candidates, most of who will only be passively on the market (see Appendix B: A Look behind the Numbers).

Pothole #5:

In a Hurry to Hire

Having to replace any member of the executive team due to an unexpected resignation is a big pain. Having to replace your CFO is a doubly big pain because typically in owner-managed companies there isn't a lot of bench strength in the finance group, so the longer the position is open, the greater the chance of something falling off the table.

It's natural for an owner-manager to want to fill the job as soon as possible. But if you post your position online and tap into your network, the great majority of the people who respond to your posting or are referred to you are going to be unemployed.

You may think this is a good thing at first because an unemployed candidate is almost inevitably ready to start immediately. Not only do you get to bypass the time it takes to conduct a search, you also get to bypass the usual notice period of three weeks to a month an employed candidate would need to give their current employer.

I advise owner-managers to proceed with caution when contemplating hiring an unemployed financial executive for the simple reason that an unemployed person's decision-making process will sometimes be unduly influenced by factors outside of professional considerations.

Simply put, someone who's been on the street for some time and has a family to support and is getting increasingly bored and frustrated with being unemployed may be inclined to take a position they wouldn't have considered when they were previously employed. If the position you have on offer isn't on or close to that unemployed candidate's previous career path (and compensation), be very careful with how you proceed, or you may be setting yourself up for future flight risk.

Pothole #6:

Chasing the Unicorn

As much as many owner-managers are not as exacting as they could be when it comes to putting together their preferred candidate profile, some hiring authorities can be too exacting. Not only will they have a list of key criteria, but they'll also be insistent on the measure of experience the candidates have to have with key criteria: the mythical "perfect" candidate.

It's not enough that someone has some experience in their industry, they want five years or more experience in that industry. And not only do they want a candidate with ERP implementation experience, they need to be an expert with SAP. And the list goes on.

Restricting the search to perfect candidates only is counterproductive. The hiring authority is going to overlook great candidates who have some experience in all of the key criteria, just not all the experience asked for in all of the criteria. As long as the key criteria are present in some material way on the person's resumé, if they have the right personality profile they should be considered viable candidates.

Straight Answers to Real Questions:

► An Embarrassment of Riches

Question: I run a $30-million logistics company based in Brampton, Ontario, and I'm trying to fill a newly created position of Vice President of Finance. I've seen a number of candidates that I've liked quite a bit who've all had significant experience as CFOs of transportation and logistics companies.

Each of the candidates I'm considering is ostensibly as well qualified as the others for the position. Is there a way of determining who might be the best suited for the job?

Answer: In this kind of situation, it can be very instructive to get an idea of how they would approach real-life situations. Present each candidate with a hypothetical (but probable) scenario and ask them to prepare a summary of what they identify as the key issues and how they would go about addressing them. Their responses should give you an idea of their analytical process and the range of the professional tool kit they will bring to bear on future challenges they'll likely be facing as your CFO.

Appendix A
Job Descriptions

Vice President of Finance and Administration

The Vice President of Finance and Administration is responsible for all financial, accounting, administrative and IT aspects of company operations. This position reports to the President and is a key member of the executive team.

Responsibilities

Provide strategic business input from a financial perspective, including short- and long-term business plans, establishing financial metrics for business operations, and monitoring and reporting progress of financial and operational targets to the President.

Responsible for the development and management of the annual operating budget and capital budget as an extension of the organization's strategic objectives.

Develop, implement and maintain accounting and administrative policies and procedures for a wide-ranging set of activities, including financial accounting and reporting, employee relations (hiring/terminating policies) and other corporate policies.

Work with operational departments to establish accounting procedures and controls for current operations if required and for new products and initiatives.

Responsible for all treasury and cash management operations.

Oversee day-to-day accounting functions, ensuring that expected accounting outcomes are timely and accurate.

Oversee all infrastructure and administrative matters, including human resources, real estate, facility and capital equipment acquisition and maintenance.

Work closely with external auditors on audit and tax planning and compliance issues.

Oversee the information technology function, including coordination and implementation of new software or technology platforms.

Director of Finance and Administration

The Director of Finance and Administration will be a key member of the management team and reports directly to the President. This is a hands-on management position responsible for leading the teams in the following areas: finance, business planning and budgeting, human resources, administration and IT.

The Director of Finance and Administration will play a critical role in partnering with the senior leadership team in strategic decision making and helping with the overall success of the operation.

Responsibilities

Analyze and present financial reports in an accurate and timely manner; clearly communicate monthly and annual financial statements to senior management.

Coordinate and lead the annual audit process, liaise with external auditors and the finance committee of the board of directors; assess any changes necessary.

Oversee and lead the annual budgeting and planning process in conjunction with the President; administer and review all financial plans and budgets; monitor progress and changes and keep senior leadership team members abreast of the organization's financial status.

Manage organizational cash flow and forecasting.

Update and implement all necessary business policies and accounting practices; improve the finance department's overall policy and procedure manual.

Effectively communicate and present critical financial matters to the board of directors.

Oversee human resources and administration, enhancing professional development, compensation and benefits, performance evaluation, training and recruitment.

Work closely and transparently with all external partners, including third-party vendors and consultants.

Oversee administrative functions as well as facilities to ensure efficient and consistent operations as the organization scales.

Controller

This position is a key member of the management team and reports directly to the President.

Responsibilities

Maintain a documented system of accounting policies and procedures.

Oversee the operations of the accounting department, especially control systems and transaction-processing operations.

Ensure that the accounting team's organizational structure is structured to achieve the department's goals and objectives.

Ensure that accounts receivable are collected promptly.

Ensure that periodic bank reconciliations are completed.

Ensure that required debt payments are made on a timely basis.

Issue timely and complete financial statements.

Manage the production of the annual budget and forecasts.

Calculate variances from the budget and report significant issues to management.

Provide for a system of management cost reports.

Provide financial analyses as needed, in particular for capital investments, pricing decisions and contract negotiations.

Coordinate the provision of information to external auditors for the annual audit.

Monitor debt levels and compliance with debt covenants.

Comply with local, provincial and federal government reporting requirements and tax filings.

Appendix B

A Look Behind the Numbers

Throughout this book I stress the importance of looking at the entire field of potentially available candidates versus the relatively few you might normally source through referrals and job boards. Most owner-managers end up hiring the one pretty good candidate they've seen out of a field of average candidates. It's possible that the person is the right fit, but the hiring authority has no assurance that they've made the right decision because they haven't got another viable choice to consider.

If you want to find the "right fit," you need to have enough good fits to choose from. And in order to come up with a decent number of good fits, you need to be able to intelligently canvas a very large number of potential candidates.

To give you an idea of the number of potential candidates you (or your recruiter) should look at, let's conduct an imaginary search for a Director of Finance for a $50-million pet food manufacturer headquartered in Mississauga. The company has been growing rapidly and needs to revamp its systems and is going to build a new plant sometime in the next few years.

Besides all the usual criteria – CPA, experience as the top finance person, personality fit, etc. – the candidates need to come out of either the food and beverage or pharmaceutical sectors (perishable ingredients require stringent quality and inventory control), have experience implementing ERP systems and preferably have some exposure to build-outs or to large Capex project management.

According to Scott's Directories, there are 226 food and pharmaceutical manufacturers in the Greater Toronto Area with 40 employees or more (companies with 40 or more employees will have at least a Controller on the management team and more commonly a Director or VP of Finance).

If we were able to contact every single Controller, Director of Finance and Vice President of Finance of those 226 companies, we would find that approximately 22 of them would be willing to consider a move for the right opportunity (historically, 10% of financial executives are either actively or passively on the market).

A pool of 22 potential candidates is a pretty good number to start with, but that number gets smaller in a real hurry. The first filter is location. Because most manufacturers in the Greater Toronto Area are located in the Mississauga area, most of their financial executives will live in the western sections of the GTA or at least be willing to commute there. However, let's assume that about 20% of the CPAs in this pool won't make the drive to this location, so we're left with 18 potential candidates.

Of those 18 candidates, a good percentage won't go any further because they're too senior, too junior, have a spotty track record, etc.

So let's say we're left with 10 potential candidates who are at the right level, have decent resumés, are knowledgeable of food or pharma manufacturing and are good with the location. The next filter is technical – how many of that number are going to have the requisite systems skills and/or have experience with build-outs or large Capex project management?

Last and not least, you still need to select for personality fit, management style and so forth.

If this was your company, and you (or your recruiter) were to go through this exercise, you would find yourself interviewing four or five very good candidates with most if not all of the criteria on your wish list. All other things being equal, the process would result in a very successful hire.

Because no matter who you ended up hiring, you would feel confident that the chosen person was the right fit because you had interviewed a decent number of good fits.

Appendix C

How to Hold Your Recruiter Accountable

In most walks of business, the customer has a pretty good idea of what to expect from the service provider, whether that provider is an internal resource or an outside supplier. If you go to your in-house counsel for advice on a contract, you can be reasonably confident that the opinion your lawyer offers represents current and relevant legal precedent. When you engage a firm of chartered accountants at year end, you actually see the audit team ensconced in your boardroom for weeks on end surrounded by last year's financial records. And when you finally receive your audited financial statements and the accompanying bill, both go into some detail as to what exactly was involved to produce those statements.

Unlike the practice of law or accountancy, the recruitment process is often quite opaque and companies that rely on in-house or outside recruiters don't always know if they're getting what they're paying for.

In order to judge if you're getting value for your money from your recruitment process, you need to look at the three key components that go into that process:

1. *The size of the field of available potential candidates.*

2. *The method used to approach potential candidates.*

3. *The ability to select and identify the best candidates.*

The first two components can be objectively quantified, while the last one is a bit more of a judgment call. Regardless, all three components of the recruitment process can be measured and managed by the hiring authority.

Size of Field

The field of potential candidates for any executive search comprises people who are actively looking for a new position and those who are relatively content but would consider another opportunity if it were compelling enough.

Active candidates peruse job boards, pro-actively network and are usually on file with a few different recruitment firms. Recruiting active candidates is relatively quick and easy, but what most hiring authorities don't realize is that active candidates represent only 15% to 20% of the potential candidates available.

The largest field of potential candidates on any search is made up of passive candidates. Passive candidates can usually be characterized as people who are gainfully employed and relatively content where they are but know that they'll need to move sometime in the next couple of years in order to advance their career. They don't make a habit of scanning job boards, usually don't have an up-to-date resumé and are rarely on file with a recruiter.

Even though passive candidates outnumber active candidates by a factor of about 6 to 1, many recruiters, both in-house and external, tend to spend their selecting from the active candidate pool to make up their short lists. They usually give a nod to the passive candidate pool and do some recruiting in this space, but if they can put together an adequate short list from the people they know to be actively looking, that tends to be very hard to resist. The problem with this, of course, is that very few hiring authorities give their recruiter a mandate to find them an "adequate" candidate.

The size of the field of candidates being approached on any given position is the single biggest determinate of success in recruiting. The more people that are considered, the more choice the hiring authority has. The more choice one has, the better decision one makes. The only way a hiring authority can ensure that they make the best possible choice is to ensure that the entire field of potential candidates, active and passive, is being considered.

Approach Methodology

Any recruiter's mantra should be: "Active candidates *may* be approached passively. Passive candidates *must* be approached actively."

A passive approach is any recruitment channel or methodology that does not involve an actual conversation between the recruiter and the potential candidate. This includes job boards, e-mail blasts, media advertisements, etc.

Why a passive approach is acceptable to attract active candidates should be fairly obvious. Anyone actively looking for a new position will regularly scan the job boards and will be pro-actively networking. They will almost always take notice of recruiters' e-mail blasts and position postings and send in their resumés.

Passive candidates do not typically respond to a passive approach for a few reasons. Reason number one is that they're not as highly motivated as their active peers, so they're not plugged into the job market, and most postings and e-mail blasts never hit their radar screen. The second reason is that unlike active candidates, they're not geared up for the recruitment process. They usually don't have an up-to-date resumé and since they're still very much committed to their current position, they're disinclined to take the time to respond to anything that isn't compelling (and most job postings and e-mail blasts are not that compelling, no matter how well-written). And last, but certainly not least, if a passive candidate is going to explore a new opportunity, they're going to want to do that on a very confidential basis. They're not going to send their resumé to someone that they don't know and trust.

A recruiter needs to have an in-depth conversation with the passive candidate detailing what exactly the opportunity entails and how it may be (or may not be) something that person would want to pursue. This is the only sure-fire way of attracting these people.

There is a step between passive and active recruitment – approaching someone specifically and directly by e-mail or LinkedIn InMail. Although this is better than most passive recruitment channels, unless you already have some previous connection to the person you're approaching, it's still not as powerful or as effective as an actual conversation.

Identifying the Best

A much as every recruiter talks about "the right fit," how do you know that they're qualified to determine what the right fit actually is? Properly mapping out and approaching the field of potential candidates is the science of the recruitment process. Being able to intelligently interview interested candidates and identify the people that are the best fit for a position is the art.

The obvious part of "fit" is technical. Whoever's putting together the short list has to know the technical component of the position they're recruiting for well enough to look past the obvious and be able to really drill down to determine whether the people they're meeting have the technical competencies to do the job. Knowing the technical component is especially important when recruiting outside of a client's particular industry. To use a horticultural analogy, it's relatively easy to fill a position in an apple orchard if you're recruiting candidates from other apple orchards, especially if they're the same relative size and complexity as your client's apple orchard. It takes a much deeper understanding of agronomy and the mechanics of fruit harvesting to recognize the right fit if you end up interviewing someone from a vineyard or a citrus grove.

The not-so-obvious part of "fit" is matching up the personalities, making sure there is a cultural fit and assessing whether the client's opportunity and the candidate's potential and ambition are in sync. This is usually a function of the length and depth of experience of the recruiter conducting the search.

There's no sure-fire way of assessing if your recruiter really understands what the "right fit" is for any search until you actually give them the assignment. However, you can quantify how well they understand the fit equation relatively early in the process – ask to meet a benchmark candidate. The recruiter should be able to identify a candidate who's a pretty close fit early in the search to use as a benchmark – something to compare what the client is expecting to what the recruiter believes is the right fit. Hopefully, they're the same thing. Sometimes they're not. So once you meet a benchmark candidate, you'll either confirm that the recruiter gets it or you'll have the opportunity to make adjustments before you get too far into the search.

Quality guru W. Edwards Deming taught that if inputs and process were inspected properly, outputs could be better predicted and inspected less. In recruitment, defining the search properly and mapping out the entire field of potential candidates is the input. Intelligently approaching those people and assessing interested candidates is the process.

Both of these functions can and should be inspected by the client. That's how the hiring authority ensures that the short list (output) they're expecting is what they actually end up getting.

Appendix D

A Better Model for Recruiting CFOs – Osborne Financial Search

The advent of new technologies and especially technologies that promote information sharing have dramatically altered the way business is done today versus 30 years ago. Today, the incredible extent and speed of information sharing has changed how most companies, and especially companies involved in the knowledge economy, conduct their business.

Recruitment firms have changed as well, but not as fast and not as far as other information-based service companies. Back in 1986, any recruitment firm's claim to fame in its particular market was the size and quality of its network. Many firms just talked the talk but some firms spent considerable time and money in building and maintaining a database of potential candidates that they could access on their clients' behalf.

These internally generated databases were strictly proprietary and jealously guarded by their owners. And because these databases were both expensive and relatively rare, recruitment firms could reasonably justify charging fees of 25% and 30% of the starting salary.

That Was Then; This Is Now

Online recruitment tools such as LinkedIn have dramatically decreased the cost of candidate research and recruitment, supplanting recruitment firms' proprietary databases and the justification for high "success" fees.

A New Model for Recruiting Financial Executives

We've developed a value-for-money-based recruitment strategy for financial executives that takes the guesswork out of the hiring process. Our clients know at the beginning of each search what the engagement is going to cost, how long it's going to take and what the expected outcomes will be.

Our strategy takes advantage of the cost effectiveness of online recruitment tools and couples it with our extensive market knowledge of the finance and accounting market. We charge on an hourly rate basis and the end fee is a function of how much time and effort we need to invest in the project, not the remuneration of the candidate hired. In every case, the client receives the short list they asked for and the fee charged will be significantly less than what they would pay a traditional recruitment firm.

Like any other professional services firm, the work we perform is completely documented, transparent and accountable to our clients. We want our clients to hire the right candidate, and we want them to have the assurance that they've hired the best candidate possible.

If you would like more information on our firm, email me at **lance@osbornefinancialsearch.com** or call me at **416 567-7782**.

Appendix E

Search Profile Worksheet

Operational Considerations

Current threats and opportunities in the business:

1. _____

2. _____

3. _____

Anticipated future threats and opportunities in the business:

1. _____

2. _____

3. _____

Areas for improvement within the finance function:

1. _____

2. _____

3. _____

Current revenue: _____

Anticipated revenue in five years: _____

Anticipated percentage growth: _____

Future Projects

Systems: _____

New products: _____

New markets: _____

New facilities: _____

Capital expenditures: _____

Financings: _____

Desired Outcomes and Candidate Criteria

Short-term desired outcomes:

    1. _____

    2. _____

    3. _____

    4. _____

Five-year desired outcomes:

    1. _____

    2. _____

3. _____

4. _____

Critical criteria:

1. _____

2. _____

3. _____

4. _____

5. _____

Desirable criteria:

1. _____

2. _____

3. _____

4. _____

5. _____